STRESS MANAGEMENT OF OLD AGE

Ankit Patel

(M.A, Clinical Psychology, SP University, VVN)

Introduction:

What is a Stress?

Stress is a person's response to a stressor such as an environmental condition or a stimulus. Stress is a body's method of reacting to a challenge. According to the stressful event, the body's way to respond to stress is by sympathetic nervous system activation which results in the fight-or-flight response. Stress typically describes a negative condition or a positive condition that can have an impact on a person's mental and physical well-being. The term *stress* had none of its contemporary connotations before the 1920s. It is a form of the Middle English *destresse*, derived via Old French from the Latin *stringere*, "to draw tight." The word had long been in use in physics to refer to the internal distribution of a force exerted on a material body, resulting in strain. In the 1920s and 1930s biological and psychological circles occasionally used the term to refer to a mental strain or to a harmful environmental agent that could cause illness. Walter Cannon used it in 1926 to refer to external factors that disrupted what he called homeostasis. But, Stress as an explanation of lived experience is absent from both lay and expert life narratives before the 1930s".

Homeostasis is a concept central to the idea of stress. In biology, most biochemical processes strive to maintain equilibrium, a steady state that exists more as an ideal and less as an achievable condition. Environmental factors, internal or external stimuli, continually disrupt homeostasis; an organism's present condition is a state in constant flux moving about a homeostatic point that is that organism's optimal condition for living. Factors causing an organism's condition to diverge too far from homeostasis can be experienced as stress. A life-threatening situation such as a physical insult or prolonged starvation can greatly disrupt homeostasis. On the other hand, an organism's effortful attempt at restoring conditions back to or near homeostasis, often consuming energy and natural resources, can also be interpreted as stress. In such instances, an organism's fight-or-flight response recruits the body's energy stores and focuses attention to overcome the challenge at hand.

The ambiguity in defining this phenomenon was first recognized by Hans Selye (1907-1982) in 1926. In 1951 a commentator loosely summarized Selye's view of stress as something that "...in addition to being itself, was also the cause of itself, and the result of itself." First to use the term in a biological context, Selye continued to define stress as "the non-specific response of the body to any demand placed upon it". As of 2011 neuroscientists such as Bruce McEwen and Jaap Koolhaas believe that stress, based on years of empirical research, "should be restricted to conditions where an environmental demand exceeds the natural regulatory capacity of an organism". Despite the numerous definitions given to stress, homeostasis appears to lie at its core.

Stress Symptoms:

Cognitive Symptoms

1. Memory problems
2. Inability to concentrate
3. Poor judgment
4. Negative behaviour
5. Anxious or racing thoughts
6. Constant worrying or feeling of insecurity

Physical Symptoms

1. Aches and pains
2. Diarrhea or constipation

3. Nausea, dizziness
4. Chest pain, rapid heartbeat
5. Loss of sex drive
6. Frequent illness

Behavioral Symptoms

1. Eating too much or too little
2. Drug/ Alcohol/ smoking abuse
3. Frequent crying
4. Social Withdrawal
5. Sudden angry outburst
6. Relationship problems

Causes of Stress:

- Major life changes
- Work / Job
- Relationship difficulties
- Inability to accept uncertainty
- Pessimism
- Negative self-talk
- Poor Health of self or relative
- Financial problems
- Being too busy
- Children and family
- Unrealistic expectations
- Perfectionism
- Pollution
- Lack of assertiveness

Need of Stress Reliever

Stress is among the leading causes of disability worldwide (WHO). Stress can be defined broadly as inability of body to maintain balance or struggling to find a balance among the multitude of challenges in one's busy life.

It is a negative condition caused by conglomeration of concerns that impacts on one's mental and physical well-being. Stress symptoms can affect our body, our thoughts, feelings, and our behavior and we might not realize it till it starts causing major damage to your health, your mood, your productivity, your relationships, and your quality of life. Stress means different to different people and can be briefly defined as experiencing

- Worry or Anxiety

- Bodily or Mental Tension

- Strain or Overwork

Stress directly affects nervous system, endocrine system and immune system of the body which causes hypertension, depression, obesity and appearance of symptoms like fatigue, lack of energy, increased heart rate, slow digestion, tensed muscles, nervousness, and sleeplessness, irritable or angry behavior. Altered immune response appears as frequent attack of cold, influenza and viral infections.

Consequence of Stress:

Long-term exposure to stress can lead to serious health problems. Chronic stress disrupts nearly every system in the body.

Major health problems are caused or exacerbated by stress are as follows;

1. Immune suppression (vulnerable to infections)
2. Hypertension (increased heart rate)
3. Diabetes
4. Pain (backache,migraine)
5. Tensed muscles
6. Digestive problem (Diarrhea or constipation)
7. Sleep problems
8. Obesity
9. Infertility
10. Speed up the aging process
11. Anxiety and depression
12. Irritability and/or angry behavior
13. Skin problems (acne,psoriasis,eczema)
14. Hair loss

About Stress management:

Stress management refers to the wide spectrum of techniques and psychotherapies aimed at controlling a person's levels of stress, especially chronic stress, usually for the purpose of improving everyday functioning. In this context, the term 'stress' refers only to a stress with significant negative consequences, or distress in the terminology advocated by Hans Selye, rather than what he calls eustress, a stress whose consequences are helpful or otherwise positive. Stress produces numerous symptoms which vary according to persons, situations, and severity. These can include physical health decline as well as depression. The process of stress management is named as one of the keys to a happy and successful life in modern society. Although life provides numerous demands that can prove difficult to handle, stress management provides a number of ways to manage anxiety and maintain overall well-being. Despite stress often being thought of as a subjective experience, levels of stress are readily measureable using various physiological tests, similar to those used in polygraphs.

Many practical stress management techniques are available, some for use by health practitioners and others for self-help, which may help an individual to reduce stress, provide positive feelings of being in control of one's life and promote general well-being.

The effectiveness of the different stress management techniques can be difficult to assess, as few of them have received significant attention from researchers. Consequently, the amount and quality of evidence for the various techniques varies widely. Some are accepted as effective treatments for use in psychotherapy, whilst others with less evidence favoring them are considered alternative therapies. Many professional organizations exist to promote and provide training in conventional or alternative therapies. There are several models of stress management, each with distinctive explanations of mechanisms for controlling stress. Much more research is necessary to provide a better understanding of which mechanisms actually operate and are effective in practice.

Transactional model:

Richard Lazarus and Susan Folkman suggested in 1984 that stress can be thought of as resulting from an "imbalance between demands and resources" or as occurring when "pressure exceeds one's perceived ability to cope". Stress management was developed and premised on the idea that stress is not a direct response to a stressor but rather one's resources and ability to cope mediate the stress response and are amenable to change, thus allowing stress to be controllable.

Among the many stressors mentioned by employees, these are the most common:

- The way employees are treated by their bosses/supervisors or company
- Lack of job security
- Company policies
- Coworkers who don't do their fair share
- Unclear expectations
- Poor communication
- Not enough control over assignments
- Inadequate pay or benefits
- Urgent deadlines
- Too much work
- Long Hours
- Uncomfortable physical conditions
- Relationship conflicts
- Coworkers making careless mistakes
- Dealing with rude customers
- Lack of cooperation
- How the company treats coworkers

In order to develop an effective stress management programmed it is first necessary to identify the factors that are central to a person controlling his/her stress, and to identify the intervention methods which effectively target these factors. Lazarus and Folkman's interpretation of stress focuses on the transaction between people and their external environment (known as the Transactional Model). The model contends that stress may not be a stressor if the person does not perceive the stressor as a threat but rather as positive or even challenging. Also, if the person possesses or can use adequate coping skills, then stress may not actually be a result or develop because of the stressor. The model proposes that people can be taught to manage their stress and cope with their stressors. They may learn to change their perspective of the stressor and provide them with the ability and confidence to improve their lives and handle all of types of stressors.

Techniques:

High demand levels load the person with extra effort and work. A new time schedule is worked up, and until the period of abnormally high, personal demand has passed, the normal frequency and duration of former schedules is limited.

Many techniques cope with the stresses life brings. Some of the following ways induce a lower than usual stress level, temporarily, to compensate the biological tissues involved; others face the stressor at a higher level of abstraction:

- Autogenic training
- Social activity
- Cognitive therapy
- Conflict resolution
- Cranial Release Technique
- Exercise
- Getting a hobby
- Meditation
- Mindfulness (psychology)
- Deep breathing
- Yoga Nidra
- Nootropics
- Reading novels
- Prayer
- Relaxation techniques
- Artistic expression
- Fractional relaxation
- Progressive relaxation
- Spas
- Somatic training
- Spending time in nature
- Stress balls
- Natural medicine
- Clinically validated alternative treatments
- Time management
- Planning and decision making

- Listening to certain types of relaxing music
- Spending quality time with pets

Techniques of stress management will vary according to the philosophical paradigm.

Stress Management Programs in Workplace:

Many businesses today have begun to use Stress Management Programs for employees who are having trouble adapting to stress at the workplace or at home. Many people have spill over stress from home into their working environment. There are a couple of ways businesses today try to alleviate stress on their employees. One way is individual intervention. This starts off by monitoring the stressors in the individual. After monitoring what causes the stress, next is attacking that stressor and trying to figure out ways to alleviate them in any way. Developing social support is vital in individual intervention, being with others to help you cope has proven to be a very effective way to avoid stress. Avoiding the stressors all together is the best possible way to get rid of stress but that is very difficult to do in the workplace. Changing behavioral patterns, May in turn, help reduce some of the stress that is put on at work as well.

Employee Assistance Programs can include in-house counseling programs on managing stress. Evaluative research has been conducted on EAPs that teach individual stress control and inoculation techniques such as relaxation, biofeedback, and cognitive restructuring. Studies show that these programs can reduce the level of physiological arousal associated with high stress. Participants who master behavioral and cognitive stress-relief techniques report less tension, fewer sleep disturbances, and an improved ability to cope with workplace stressors.

Another way of reducing stress at work is by simply changing the workload for an employee. Some may be too overwhelmed that they have so much work to get done, or some also may have such little work that they are not sure what to do with themselves at work. Improving communications between employees also sounds like a simple approach, but it is very effective for helping reduce stress. Sometimes making the employee feel like they are a bigger part of the company, such as giving them a voice in bigger situations shows that you trust them and value their opinion. Having all the employees mesh well together is a very underlying factor which can take away much of workplace stress. If employees fit well together and feed off of each other, the chances of lots of stress are very minimal. Lastly, changing the physical qualities of the workplace may reduce stress. Changing simple things such as the lighting, air temperature, odor, and up to date technology.

Intervention is broken down into three steps: Primary, Secondary, Tertiary. Primary deals with eliminating the stressors all together. Secondary deals with detecting stress and figuring out ways to cope with it and improving stress management skills. Finally, tertiary deals with recovery and rehabbing the stress all together. These three steps are usually the most effective way to deal with stress not just in the workplace, but overall.

Objectives:

The objectives of the present study are such...

1. Main aim of this study is to know about the old age from join family and old age home groups' stress management.
2. To know about the old person' present life style of two different groups (Join family and Old age home)
3. To study and compare the stress management of old male and female from join family group.
4. To study and compare the stress management of old male and female from old age home group.
5. To know the difference between the stress of join family and old age home groups' old males and females.
6. Massage to whole society that all old persons require more sympathy, co-operation, affection, love and care.

Hypothesis:

The following null hypothesis is stated for the present investigation...

1. There is no significant effect of stress management level of old male and female of join family group.
2. There is no significant effect of stress management level of old male and female of old age home group.
3. There is no significant effect of stress management level of old males from join family and old age home groups.
4. There is no significant effect of stress management level of old females from join family and old age home groups.
5. There is no significant effect of stress management level of old males and females.

Variables:

In present research following variables are shown in this table

Name of Variable	Nature of Variable	Number of Variable
Two* Groups	IV	03
Stress management	DV	04
Gender	IV	02

IV = Independent Variable, DV = Dependent Variable, *Join family and Old age home*

Sampling:

Group	Male	Female	Total
Join family	25	25	50
Old age home	25	25	50
-	-	-	-
Total	50	50	100

Tools:

In the present study for finding of stress management level on the old persons the main objectives of this research. Researcher has developed stress management progress report of research sample variable of old males and females from MAHISAGAR district area. Percentage score present study is for finding out the "**STRESS MANAGEMENT QUESTIONNAIRE (SMQ)**" test developed by Dr. Jim Petersen (1976). He is an Arizona psychologist specializing in helping people with stress and stress related disorders at his Biofeedback and Stress Management Clinic develop a stress assessment tool called the Stress Management Questionnaire (SMQ). The SMQ was designed to help individuals identify potential stress "risk" areas and, then, based upon the results develop an intervention programs to reduce stress and enhance one's stress mastery skills.

The initial SMQ worked well but needed to be refined, shortened and psychometrically validated. A shorter version of the SMQ was developed. It proved to be easier to use and produced even better results. The first successful application of the SMQ was in the University of Arizona's "Project Well Aware about Health" program funded by the Kellogg Foundation (1980). Since then, the SMQ has helped thousands of stressed

In 1980, the SMQ underwent a comprehensive validation study funded by the National Institute for Occupational Safety and Health (NIOSH). Using stratified random sampling techniques with several major corporations, the result was the identification of seven key behavioral "risk" factors or scales.
Because stress is known to have a negative effect on one's body and health, a follow-up study was then conducted to determine if the seven primary scales correlated with any negative effects of stress.

The SMQ is a 34 page booklet complete with the 87 basic SMQ questions, a scoring and profiling section and detailed information about each of the stress "risk" scores. The SMQ Booklet can be used by an individual for self-exploration or as part of a small or large group stress management training program. The SMQ is flexible training booklets that assess participants' stress levels, provides a profile of their results and gives solid professional information about how to develop stress mastery knowledge, skills and attitudes.

Research Design:

For present study SMQ test was used. The test is taken from www.Stressmaster.com website (3219 E. Camelback Rd. #140 Phoenix, AZ 85018 480-444-630 • Skype "TheStressmaster"). This test measures Stress level. In this research, I have discussed above old males and females from two different groups' stress level.

100 old persons (Male and Female) were selected randomly MAHISAGAR district area' join families and old age homes. Old persons were divided in two groups. Group one 'Join family', in which 50 persons (25 are male and 25 are female). Number of two' group 'Old Age Home', in which 50 persons (25 are males and 25 are females).

After collecting the date statistical analysis was done according to key for the comparison of different groups 't' test was calculated.

Results and Discussion:

Table no.1: Male and female from join family group.

Group	N	Mean	SD	SEM	t	Level
Male	25	35.84	4.37	0.87	0.2856	NS
Female	25	36.36	7.98	1.60		0.01

- This table indicates no significant difference between male and female from join family group. Females are more effective in stress management.

Table no. 2: Male and female from old age home group.

Group	N	Mean	SD	SEM	t	Level
Male	25	36.56	5.59	1.12	1.0718	NS
Female	25	37.92	3.00	0.60		0.01

- This table indicates no significant difference between male and female from old age home group. Females are more effective in stress management.

Table no.3: Males from *old age home and **join family groups.

Group	N	Mean	SD	SEM	t	Level
Male*	25	36.56	5.59	1.12	0.5071	NS
Male**	25	35.84	4.37	0.87		0.01

- : Here also no significant difference is found in males from Join family and old age home group. Males of old age home are more effective in stress management.

Table no.4: Females from *old age home and **join family groups.

Group	N	Mean	SD	SEM	t	Level
Female*	25	37.92	3.00	0.60	0.9146	NS
Female**	25	36.36	7.98	1.60		0.01

- : Here also no significant difference is found in females from Join family and old age home group. Females of old age home are more effective in stress management.

Table no.4: All over Males and Females.

Group	N	Mean	SD	SEM	t	Level
Male	50	36.20	4.98	0.70	0.8506	NS
Female	50	37.14	6.02	0.85		0.01

- This table indicates no significant difference between male and female. Females are more effective in stress management.

Charts:

1. **Male and female from join family group.**

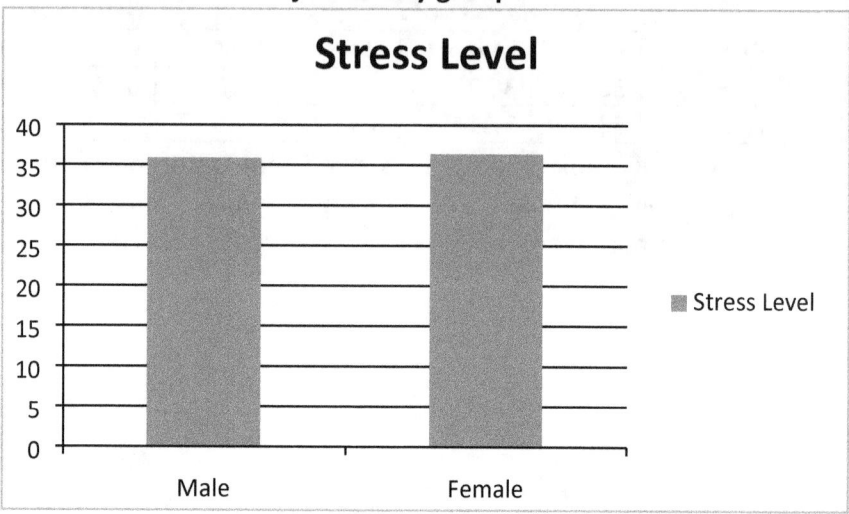

2. **Male and female from old age home group.**

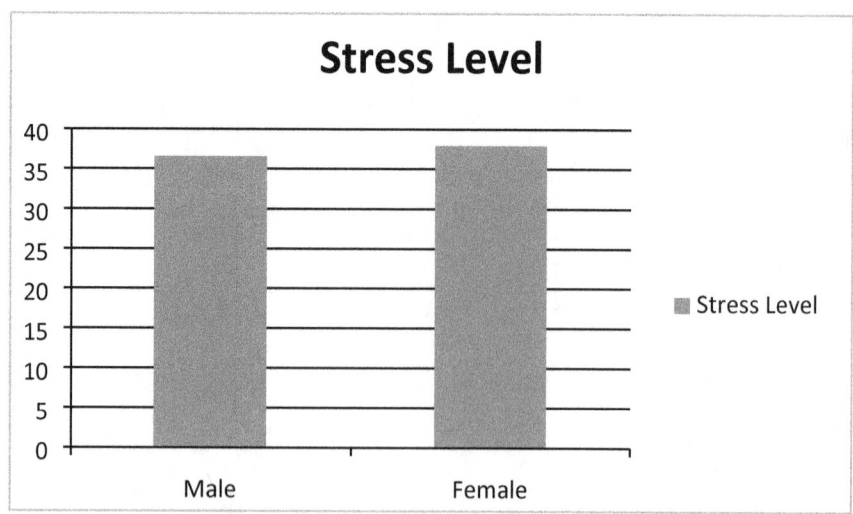

3. Males from *old age home and **join family groups.

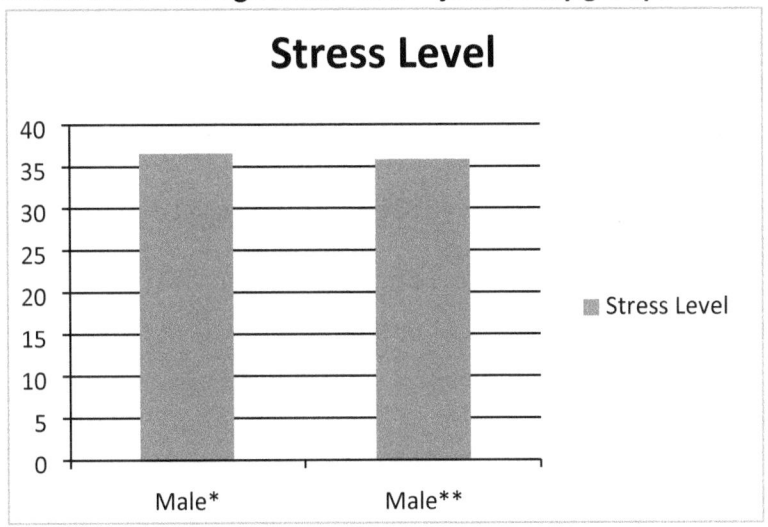

4. Females from *old age home and **join family groups.

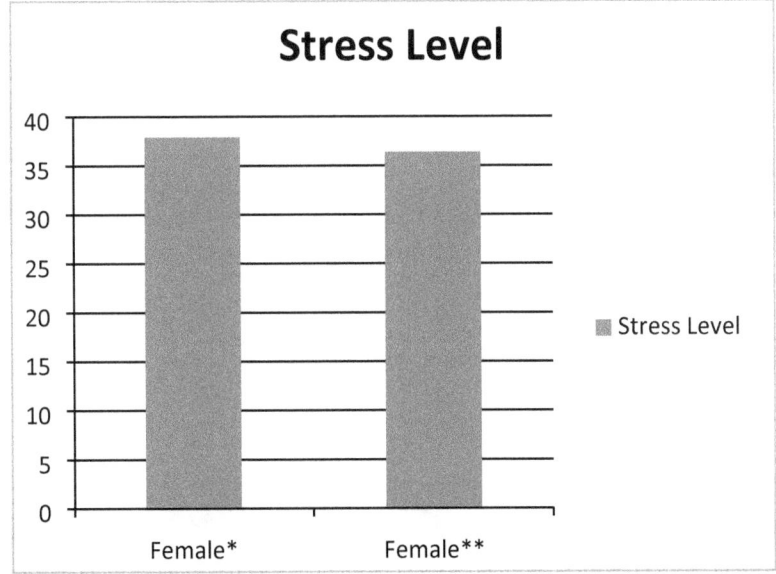

5. **Table no.4: All over Males and Females.**

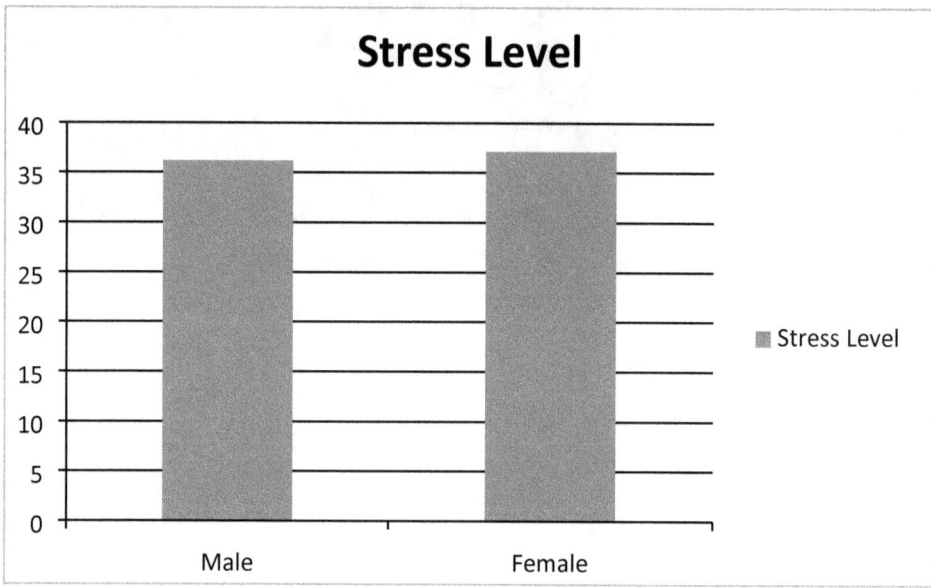

Interpretation of Tables and Testing of Hypothesis:

- HO1: There is no significant effect of Stress management level between old male and female of join family group. Tested t value is 0.2856 at 0.01 levels. So, we accepted of this null hypothesis.
- HO2: There is no significant effect of Stress management level between old male and female of old age home group. Tested t value is 1.0718 at 0.01 levels. So, we accepted of this null hypothesis.
- HO3: There is no significant effect of Stress management level between old males of join family and old age home group. Tested t value is 0.5071 at 0.01 levels. So, we accepted of this null hypothesis.
- HO4: There is no significant effect of Stress management level between old female of join family and old age home group. Tested t value is 0.9146 at 0.01 levels. So, we accepted of this null hypothesis.
- HO5: There is no significant effect of Stress management level between old males and females. Tested t value is 0.8506 at 0.01 levels. So, we accepted of this null hypothesis.

Finding:

- There is no significant of stress management level of between male and female in join family group.
- There is no significant of stress management level of between male and female in old age home group.
- Females are more effective in stress management compare to males.
- Old age home group is more effective in stress management compare to join family group.
- Old age home's old person to done effective stress management compare to joint family because these old person connected to each other and shared own problems, emotions and sympathy etc.

Reference:

1. Paul Susic MA Licensed Psychologist, Ph.D Candidate. "Stress Management: What can you do?". St. Louis Psychologists and Counseling Information and Referral. Retrieved February 5, 2013.
2. Cannon, W. (1939). The Wisdom of the Body, 2nd ed., NY: Norton Pubs.
3. Selye, H (1950). "Stress and the general adaptation syndrome". Br. Med. J. 1 (4667): 1383-92.
4. Lazarus, R.S., & Folkman, S. (1984). Stress, Appraisal and Coping. New York: Springer.

5. Somaz, Wenk Heidi & Tulgan, Bruce (2003). Performance under Pressure: Managing Stress in the Workplace.Canada. HRD Press Inc.p 7-8. ISBN 0-87425-741-7

6. Mills, R.C. (1995). *Realizing Mental Health: Toward a new Psychology of Resiliency.* Sulberger & Graham Publishing, Ltd. ISBN 0-945819-78-1

7. Sedgeman, J.A. (2005). Health Realization/Innate Health: Can a quiet mind and a positive feeling state is accessible over the lifespan without stress-relief techniques? Med. Sci. Monitor 11(12) HY47-52.

8. Lehrer, Paul M.; David H. (FRW) Barlow, Robert L. Woolfolk, Wesley E. Sime (2007). *Principles and Practice of Stress Management, Third Edition.* pp. 46–47. ISBN 1-59385-000-X.

9. Cohen, S; Janicki-Deverts, D; Miller, GE. (2007). "Psychological Stress and Disease". *JAMA* **298** (14): 1685–1687.

10. Pinquart, M., & Sörensen, S. (2003). Differences between caregivers and noncaregivers in psychological health and physical health: a meta-analysis. Psychology and aging, 18(2), 250.

11. Margaret E. Kemeny, "The Psychobiology of Stress" in Current Directions in Psychological Science Vol. 12, No. 4 (Aug., 2003), pp. 124-129.

12. Kobasa, S. C. (1982). The Hardy Personality: Toward a Social Psychology of Stress and Health. In G. S. Sanders & J. Suls (Eds.), Social Psychology of Health and Illness (pp. 1-25). Hillsdale, NJ: Lawrence Erlbaum Assoc.

13. Uchino, B. N. (2009). Understanding the links between social support and physical health: A life-span perspective with

emphasis on the reparability of perceived and received support. Perspectives on Psychological Science, 4(3), 236-255.

14. Berkman, L. F., Glass, T., Brissette, I., & Seeman, T. E. (2000). From social integration to health: Durkheim in the new millennium. Social science & medicine, 51(6), 843-857.

15. Cohen, S., & Wills, T. A. (1985). Stress, social support, and the buffering hypothesis. Psychological bulletin, 98(2), 310.